THE LIFE OF THE GIRAFFE

THE LIFE OF THE GIRAFFE

by Bradley Smith   A Gemini Smith Book
Photographs by Bradley Smith and Jerry Cooke

HAMLYN
London • New York • Sydney • Toronto

Photography: Bradley Smith and Jerry Cooke
Graphics: Douglas Armstrong
Editorial Research: Helen Paula Smith
Editorial Assistants: Florence Kronfeld
                     Janet Goldstein
                     Carol Kerr

Published by the Hamlyn Publishing Group Limited
London • New York • Sydney • Toronto
Hamlyn House, Feltham, Middlesex, England
and published as a Gemini Smith book in the U.S.A.
Copyright © Gemini Smith, Incorporated and
the Hamlyn Publishing Group Limited 1972
ISBN 0 600 35454 7
Printed in Hong Kong by Toppan

Behind a thorn tree, on the equatorial plains of Africa, a young giraffe twists its neck to nurse.

From a small, horned, deer-like creature of thirty-five million years ago the modern giraffe has become a tree-top tall, peaceful animal. It is one of the few wild mammals whose existence is not yet seriously threatened by man.

(overleaf) In a show of affection a mother nuzzles her older calf. The younger waits to nurse. ▷

△ *Separated by high grasses the giraffe family, with their long necks, can easily keep in touch.*

Only a few weeks old this baby giraffe is six feet tall. It weighs as much as a full-grown man. ▷

A giraffe taking a nap is unusual. They never sleep lying down more than five minutes at a time.

In a regal posture a juvenile giraffe sibly a year and a half old) waits for his mother.

Giraffes are the easiest animals to spot on the plains of Kenya. These may not be in the same family. Necks raised like periscopes two giraffes look over a tangle of trees in Amboseli National Reserve.

MEET THE GIRAFFE

If you had never seen a giraffe but only read a description of one, it would be hard to believe such an animal could exist. Not even an imagined outer-space creature has so fantastic an appearance as the giraffe. With enormous eyes like a telescope lens which can see front, side and rear, and a long flexible neck rising like a periscope from a submarine to survey the entire countryside, the giraffe is one of the most specialized creatures living on our earth today. It is not only its amazing eyesight nor its 16 to 18 foot height that makes the giraffe unique. This incredible beast has a skin patterned like the leopard (except that the spots are shaped either like leaves or squares), its babies are born six feet tall, it runs twice as fast as a man, and it can kill a lion or a hyena with one well-placed kick.

It took the giraffe a long time to get its name. The Greeks called it the *camelopardalis*. They arrived at this misnomer through the observations of early Greek naturalists who believed that the strange beast was the offspring produced by the mating of a camel with a leopard. This name continued and was even used by the famous Swedish professor, Carolus Linnaeus, who named and classified as many animals and plants as he could during his lifetime. He classified the giraffe with the deer and called it *Cervus camelopardalis*. But the Greek name was too long to be popular and it is probable that many observers doubted it really sprang from

the leopard and the camel. The early Arabs called the animal a *zarafah*. They most likely got the word from the Ethiopian *zarat* which means thin or slender.

Finally, it came to be recognized as a distinct genus by a French zoologist, Mathurin Jacques Brisson, in 1756. As a reward he got his name added to it. The scientific name today is *Giraffa camelopardalis Brisson*, but it is known throughout the world as a giraffe. The giraffe has an even number of toes, therefore it falls into the order called *Artiodactyla*. Because it has more than one stomach (in fact it has four) and can move its food up from its stomach to chew it a second time, it belongs to the suborder of ruminants called *Ruminantia*. Because it has at least one living relative, the okapi, it belongs to the family of *Giraffidae*. And, because it only mates with other giraffes and is therefore different from every other animal, it belongs to the genus *Giraffa*. Therefore, the giraffe is an even-toed hoofed animal which belongs to the mammal group called even-toed ungulates such as the pig and the cow. But this description is not much better than Dr. Samuel Johnson's was when he referred to it as an Abyssinian animal, taller than the elephant but not so thick. But more about the quaint and far-out descriptions of the giraffe in our chapter on its history and legends.

HOW GIRAFFES SURVIVE

The giraffe has survived because of the nature of evolution. Over hundreds of thousands of years, animals and plants acquire those characteristics which they need to continue living on the earth. The giraffe has developed, among other qualities, incredibly effective eyesight. It can see many things that are invisible to human eyes. The almond-shaped eye is much larger than that of the deer or the cow. The giraffe has an instant reaction to certain colors. A lion stalking slowly between the dry, tall grasses looks like the same color as the grasses to the human eye and, therefore, is invisible. However, the giraffe can distinguish between the different color values of the lion's coat and the grasses and therefore can see him.

In appearance the giraffe's eye is alert and seems to reflect a quick intelligence. The muscles controlling the eye allow it to wink on either side. This means that when dust or sand is blowing the giraffe can close one eye and keep the other one open. Its eyelashes are dark and long. When the eye is closed the line of the eyelash looks like a quarter- or crescent-moon.

The long nose of the giraffe has a special feature —a muscular mechanism which can completely close its slit-like nostrils protecting it against dust. It is possible that this unique characteristic may have other functions such as keeping long thorns from scratching the inside of the nostril when the giraffe bites into the thorn tree.

Considering the size of its huge body, the giraffe has very small ears. The ear passages and the structure of the inner ear, however, are comparatively large in relation to the size of its skull. Like its eyesight, its hearing is excellent.

Among its most important survival qualities is the giraffe's ability to eat food that is out of reach of other animals or so covered with sharp thorns or prickles that only he, with his special eating equipment, can consume it. How then does the giraffe eat? First, it uses its lips, teeth and tough, long (18 inches) sinuous tongue to gather the food into its mouth. In an automatic reflex, the tongue spits out sharp thorns and insects. What remains is briefly chewed, swallowed and goes into the first stomach, called the rumen. There strong digestive juices go to work on it. Now the giraffe can bring it up into its mouth and rechew it. For hundreds of years this process has been called "chewing the cud." It really means rechewing the food. From the Latin word *rumin* comes the more common verb ruminate, which means to ponder or reflect. This is just the effect the giraffe gives as it slowly moves its jaw back and forth.

This complicated digestive apparatus is necessary for the giraffe is a herbivorous animal, which means it feeds chiefly on leaves, tree bark and plants. It spends considerable time eating because it requires hundreds of pounds of food to supply its needs. Carnivorous, or meat-eating, animals spend

Giraffes depend upon their vision more than most animals. Their eye is larger than most mammals.

much less time finding food. They are able to catch and eat the herbivorous animals who have already converted the grasses and plants into energy producing protein. Thus, when a lion kills a young giraffe, he obtains concentrated food and is able to digest it quickly and easily.

Trees and bushes are essential to the survival of the giraffe not only' for their food value but also for their water content. This is one reason why giraffes do not have to visit the water hole as often as most animals — sometimes as seldom as once a week. For hundreds of years it was thought that the giraffe was closely related to the camel. While it needs no more water than the camel, there is actually no close connection.

The giraffe feeds in the sun while almost all other animals tend to feed in the shade. This makes it easier for giraffes to keep a wary eye out for lions and also enables them to browse over the savannas almost undisturbed. Its hide, which is approximately an inch thick, probably insulates it from the burning rays of the sun.

Giraffes feed heavily on leaves and young shoots stripping the trees up to heights of 16 to 18 feet. Because of this, the entire landscape acquires a sculptured appearance. This stripping process may contribute to the ultimate destruction of the trees by elephants unable to reach that high. The elephants in search of food must use their strength to push the trees over, ripping them up by the roots. They can then get the leaves and bark the giraffes were unable to reach.

In Kenya the giraffes enjoy a food delicacy no other animals will touch. This is the thorn bush or thorn tree, a low-lying shrub so covered with spines that all other animals avoid it. But it gives the giraffe no trouble. Its tongue and lips seem impervious to the prickles and its saliva has the consistency of soft rubber. This combination enables it to extract the nutritional value and easily eject the thorns.

The giraffe does not spend all of its time eating as some animals do probably because its periscope neck and sharp eyesight enable it to spot food at great distances. However, a full-grown male in the wild may consume a hundred pounds or more of food per day. They are very fond of bark and often denude the trees of this as well as their leaves. As they eat, they break off small branches by swinging their neck with an upward motion of the chin. It takes two full-grown giraffes less than 30 minutes to strip a large acacia tree of its leaves, branches and bark leaving only a white skeleton outlined against the sky.

The giraffe never eats grass, partly because it has a very awkward time getting its head all the way down to the ground between its forelegs, and also because it does not like grass. Adult giraffes feed at the higher tree levels while the juveniles and baby giraffes seem content to eat what they can on the lower reaches of the trees and bushes. During the writer's daily observations of the giraffes' eating habits they did not seem to take food from one another. Even a full-grown male will allow a young male or baby giraffe to eat alongside him. When he snaps off a large branch, he does not try to follow it as it falls to the ground but rather allows the younger one to strip it of leaves and bark.

COURTSHIP,
BIRTH AND BABIES

Of all the mammals the giraffe may have the most detached family organization. Solitary male giraffes rove the countryside looking for females ready for mating. His courtship is a leisurely affair as he follows the female for miles staying just as close to her as possible. The only indication that the writer has ever seen that the female is interested in the male's pursuit is the provocative hip-swinging gait she adopts as she leads him on. When she moves away she always waits for the male to catch up. He occasionally lays his neck alongside hers and bumps up against her as often as she will allow. They touch frequently in this ever-moving romance, for the female almost never stands still. As the male moves behind her, he pushes his long nose against her body.

Finally, he determines whether she is ready to mate by the taste of her urine. Few people have seen the actual mating of giraffes in the wild. Apparently they continue to move away until they are sure they are alone. And with their ability to sweep the countryside with their eyes, it is easy for them to know if they are being observed by man or beast.

The mating itself is of brief duration. The male rears up on his back legs, places his forelegs across the female's body in the same manner as the horse or dog. After mating, the male shows no interest in that particular female, whether she becomes pregnant or not.

It takes between 14 and 15 months for the female giraffe to have her calf. The young are usually born well out of sight of predatory animals for in the brief interval of birth the female and her young are unprotected. She gives birth in private, unattended by other giraffes. She must therefore stay alert for possible predators such as hyenas, lions or leopards. They are her greatest enemies at this critical time.

The giraffe gives birth while standing up and indeed she moves about continuously before dropping her young one. The baby giraffe makes a major trip into the world at birth for it drops between five and six feet from the mother to the ground. Fortunately, it is born feet first followed by the head, neck and shoulders, which are between the forelegs. Its position is like that of a diver.

When the baby is born it weighs as much as a full-grown man, between 120 and 160 pounds, and is five to six feet tall. Of all the baby animals the giraffe certainly has the roughest, most adventurous trip into the world. As soon as the baby arrives the mother begins licking it not only to clean it up but to remove the odor which can attract predators to the spot. Then she nudges it unless it is already on its feet. The young giraffe stands within minutes and is able to nurse 15 minutes after birth.

The female has four teats under her hindquarters from which the baby nurses. She supplies a very rich milk, which has seven times more protein than that of a cow but it is thick and unpalatable to human beings. Because of his long neck, the baby giraffe has to spread his legs and twist his neck sideways causing the head to be almost upside down when he reaches for his mother's milk. The mother giraffe is usually impatient with the baby nursing. Whenever she feels the calf has had enough milk, she simply strolls

Giraffes often touch each other: mothers show attention to young, and courtship is intimate.

away leaving the youngster standing with its neck out and its mouth open.

It is doubtful that the baby giraffe feeds on its mother's milk exclusively for more than its first week after birth. Unlike the human baby, or the young that are born to meat-eating animals, the giraffe can run within hours after it is born. It arrives fully coordinated. If this were not so, very few baby giraffes would survive. Evolution has afforded this kind of protection to those animals that do not hunt to survive. The meat-eating mammals must spend considerable time as nursing infants, then a learning period as juveniles before they know how to defend themselves and how to find food. Meanwhile, they have the complete protection of their parents. But the young giraffe and the mother who has just given birth are defenseless except for their ability to run away. Even so, a high percentage of baby giraffes are killed by predators. But, because so many females become pregnant and give birth every two years, the giraffe population is not becoming extinct.

Because young giraffes are able to fend for themselves, they are not always seen near their mothers while they are growing up. Yet they stay in the same neighborhood. It is possible that the giraffes' height enables them to be apart and yet know exactly where baby or mother is browsing. Smaller animals have to stay closer together because they do not have this advantage. The giraffe is able to keep a continuous visual check on the entire territory around it.

The writer has observed the mother giraffe signaling to, and rounding up, its offspring when it moves from one feeding area to another. And giraffes do sometimes nurse well into their second year although the calves are half-grown by that time, for giraffe babies grow very quickly. At birth they are six feet tall and at one year 12 feet tall. This sounds more spectacular than it really is. Human babies usually double their weight in six months and triple it in a year.

Maturity comes to the giraffe by the time it is four years old. It can then reproduce itself even though it has not yet reached full growth. The giraffe is a full-grown adult when it is seven years old. A female will probably be 15 to 16 feet tall and weigh about 2,000 pounds. A male's height will range from 16 to 18 feet and he will weigh 2,500 to 3,000 pounds.

THE LIFE OF THE HERD

Giraffe herds are rarely large. The writer has observed herds of 16 giraffes moving together but has much more often seen groups of four to 12. Some authorities have reported herds numbering 50 or more but these are extremely rare. The giraffe is not truly a herd-oriented animal. Each one seems to operate as an individual responsible for his own welfare. Even mothers cease to care for their calves before the young animal reaches two years. Indeed, a number of authorities have suggested that the mother ceases to be concerned for the young one after it is only a few weeks old.

One story told by writer-photographer Norman Myers concerns a giraffe with a young calf. The mother sailed over a fence (giraffes are great high jumpers) but, once on the other side, could not seem to understand why the calf did not follow her. She wandered up and down the fence puzzled, as the young one kept up with her on the other side of the fence. Finally, the mother, instead of jumping back over the fence to be with her calf, moved off deserting it. This does not prove that giraffes are thoughtless about their young but only that, like the horse, elephant and most mammals, they do not have much reasoning power. The problem was simply too difficult for her to solve.

Male giraffes certainly show no affection for the juveniles but they have a live-and-let-live attitude, and are not known to attack or harm calves or juveniles. There is never a feeling of a tight family group even though one sometimes sees a male, female, young calf and juvenile traveling together. One is much more likely to see two or more females with their young ones moving along and then spot a solitary male a mile or two away.

The herd life may be more compact than it looks, however, for giraffes can be in touch with each other even though they are miles apart. In other words, because giraffes are the tallest of all the animals, at their eye level there is little to block their view of each other. Therefore, their concept of space may allow them to feel close together even though separated by a considerable distance, as humans would see it. So remember, even though giraffes in the zoo are often displayed as family groups, they do not necessarily lead a close-knit family life in the wild.

Male giraffes do fight one another but they bluff a lot too. One attempts to face down the other quite often. No one is sure why they fight though it is probably over an available female who is usually so far away that the observer of the fight may never see her. The giraffe uses its head as a weapon. Although it has small horns, about which more later, they are not used for butting or goring.

As the giraffe grows older his head becomes harder and harder. He actually develops a thicker bone structure in his skull, probably because he uses it as a weapon. When males confront each other, unless one of them backs down, a fight begins. Each gets a chance to strike the other with his head and long neck. The neck is used as if it were a heavy whip with a hard object on the end. That object, of course, is the giraffe's head and it becomes a very effective weapon with the muscular swinging neck behind it. The heavy blows alternate as one animal and then the other strikes. The smack of the blows can be heard from great distances. After giving each other a thorough neck-lashing, one will finally retire leaving the other in charge. These fights are fairly common among full-grown males but are never seen among females.

The head is not often injured in any serious way during these contests for nature has taken care of the delicate internal organs by encasing the brain and nerve centers in a massive cage of bone.

Watching a herd of giraffes as they move smoothly across the plains is somewhat like seeing a small fleet of boats under sail. They seem to float rather than walk or run and each one looks a bit like a sailing vessel, its mast extending into the sky and tail waving like a flag. The giraffe moves rocking slightly as though on a rolling sea. It even looks a little like a child's rocking horse multiplied in size a dozen times. The gait can also be compared to a moving seesaw for one end of the giraffe goes up and then the other. He covers 15 feet in a stride.

The giraffe uses his neck to balance the shift in his weight as he moves. Most of its power is in its forelegs rather than in the rear, as in the horse. When the giraffe's forelegs move forward the neck moves ahead. Then, as the weight shifts to his hind legs, the neck moves back allowing the front legs to be lifted for the next stride. But as soon as the front hoofs touch the ground the neck swings back to reduce the forward motion. Unless this was so, the weight of its neck and shoulders would cause him to fall on his face.

The giraffe has three speeds forward: its slow motion walk; its pacing, which is the gait it uses most; and the gallop. It does not often gallop but, when it does, it rates near the cheetah as one of the swiftest animals alive.

In Arabia there was an often told formula for testing the speed and stamina of the horse. It could be measured by the horse's ability to catch up with a galloping giraffe. The animal that could outrun it once a day was considered excellent. But the stallion that could catch up with a giraffe twice a day was considered an extraordinary horse fit for a king.

Giraffe herds have a tendency to stay pretty much in the same location. They never migrate for long distances because they usually are able to find food in sufficient quantity in one area. Unlike most mammals they do not define their territory nor do they defend it from each other or other animals. They are placid, pleasant and peaceful.

Even the most persistent and sharp-eyed amateur viewer is unlikely to see a giraffe lying down, yet they do. This is one indication of their dependency upon each other for they never lie down to sleep unless there is another giraffe standing nearby. A giraffe sleeps lying down for a few minutes, perhaps from two to 10, with his legs tucked around him, his neck curled back, the head resting on his hip. They spend as much as a half hour out of every 24 sleeping this way, but never all at one time. For sleeping is the most dangerous thing a giraffe can do next to having a baby, because getting up on its feet is a major project. The giraffe must throw his neck back, which automatically pulls his forelegs up. He straightens them and swings his neck forward which acts as a lever to pull the back legs up. This maneuver takes time and could give a lion the opportunity to leap. So the giraffe is very careful about where and when he lies down.

The giraffe appears to live out his life in slow motion. Bulls, cows or calves are never in a hurry, yet they cover great distances in a single day, though they apparently have no destination and may even be moving around in circles. However, if it is necessary, giraffes can travel as much as a hundred miles a day. When they are just grazing they probably cover 20 to 30 miles.

The old bull giraffe may live a solitary existence yet he never seems to constitute the kind of danger to native villagers that a bull elephant does. The older males observed by the writer gave the impression of being quite tolerant and generally less nervous about humans than the females or the young ones. Curiosity is a major trait of the giraffe. They will come quite close to a land rover or a jeep, then stop, contemplate the sights around them, and remain still for as long as three minutes moving only their lower jaw as they silently rechew their food.

An airplane flying low overhead may scare a herd of antelopes but the giraffe is unimpressed. He will casually look up and then continue the important business of eating. If a plane lands, his curiosity is aroused and he is likely to walk up quite close to it while the other animals scatter.

Humans may walk within a few feet of the herd but then the giraffes move slowly away, always keeping the same distance.

In captivity giraffes become tame quite rapidly. They like to watch the passing scene around them. At Lion Country Safari, a game preserve in Southern California, giraffes wander between the automobiles occasionally licking their tops. They are especially fascinated by the huge yellow school buses, which they probably view as another form of giraffe. The giraffe keeper at Lion Country reports that they are unmanageable when they first come to the preserve and some have a tendency to kick. But, after they have been around for a few weeks, they can be handled and herded with ease.

In Nairobi National Park in Kenya, the University College at Nairobi has been keeping an eye on the giraffe herds. Among other things they have reported, after photographing hundreds of giraffes, is that the pattern of every giraffe is as unique and distinct as a person's fingerprints. Within the next few years they hope to determine much more about the daily life of the giraffe in the wild by identifying and observing the behavior of a large concentration of them over a specific period of time.

The giraffe gets along quite peacefully with the grass-eating wild animals of Africa. An elephant herd may stroll by and neither elephants nor giraffes appear to notice the presence of each other. Giraffes wander through herds of zebras, wildebeests, impalas and gazelles without any contact or conflict. Each individual keeps to himself though he may be within a herd of other animals. The herds exhibit little curiosity and seldom show signs of aggressiveness. They seem afraid only of predators and generally give the impression of having nothing to worry about.

HISTORY AND LEGENDS

There is an ancient story that the Creator of all things finished forming the animals and then found he had some left over pieces. These consisted of the skin of a leopard, the speed of an antelope and the neck and legs of a camel. He stretched the neck a bit and created the giraffe.

The long history of the giraffe begins at least 25 million years ago when it roamed over much of Europe and Asia. There were many varieties of ungulates (hoofed animals) in these ancient times, all descending from a common ancestor. Horses, deer and cattle were among them. But the *giraffids* possessed many .peculiarities. A few had longer horns than others. They varied in size from miniature to colossal. Some giraffe bones, when discovered in India, were thought to be the remains of giants. This is not as strange as it sounds. The bones of other ancient and now extinct mammals were often identified by earlier civilizations as the remains of giants they believed once inhabited the earth. Over millions of years the giraffe evolved into the animal we know today.

Man has known the giraffe for at least 7,000 years and probably much longer. Some 5,000 years before Christ he scratched images on rock formations in the middle of the Sahara Desert of an animal that can only be identified as a giraffe. These are not rough outlines but finished, detailed etchings with the horns well defined and the distinctive body pattern shown. Some of the rock engravings show giraffes with one leg caught in a primitive trap. Others are shown with halters around their necks.

But neither primitive man nor modern man ever succeeded in domesticating the giraffe. It would, of course, be a very difficult task. Just to lead a 16 to 18 foot animal around would be unwieldy. More important, he would be useless in a domesticated state except for food. The milk is undrinkable. He cannot be ridden because his back slopes so much a man would be inclined to slide down.

They were hunted for food. But primitive hunters must have had little effect upon the early giraffe herds. They could easily outrun a man and were very wary. They rarely allowed humans to approach close enough to shoot them with arrows. Nor were the kind of arrows primitive men used effective against their inch thick hide. So, except for an occasional kill, and perhaps an occasional capture, the giraffe had little trouble surviving.

With the exception of the elephant, no mammal has played a more important role in the history of the world than the giraffe. It was considered a sacred animal by the early hunters. It was the animal he chose most often when he engraved pictures on his cave dwellings and rocky ledges.

With the passage of time, the giraffe became an important symbol in civilized countries. The Egyptians decorated their pottery with outline figures of the giraffe more than 3,000 years before Christ. In early painting and sculpture of the Egyptians the giraffe is shown peacefully parading in a line of animals and men. All through early Egyptian art representations of the giraffe continued to appear. It was almost certainly related to the animal gods of early Egypt as the elephant was related to the gods of India. The Egyptians made an attempt to domesticate the giraffe, the deer and the gazelle as well. But they were no more successful than more primitive people had been.

As trade between countries became more common, giraffes were exported from North Africa to the Mediterranean and even to China. Julius Caesar proudly brought a giraffe to Rome. African potentates sent giraffes as gifts to Persia and India. The Holy Roman Emperor, Frederick II, received a giraffe as a gift from faraway admirers. They were even sent as peace offerings to the rulers of Mongolia. Marco Polo brought word back to Italy, after his famous journey to China, that the tall slender animals were known on the island of Madagascar.

It is probable that Michelangelo saw a giraffe during his lifetime. One was sent from the Sultan of Egypt to Lorenzo de Medici in 1486. This great statesman, poet and patron of the arts proudly exhibited it in his private zoo. For many succeeding generations giraffes were the pride of royal zoos throughout Europe and Asia. They became known in France as *le bel animal du roi*, the beautiful animal of the king. The honor of having bred and reared the first giraffe in Europe goes to the Zoological Society of London. This event happened only some 130 years ago.

But even before the giraffe began to travel widely the Greeks knew of him. Between 1 A.D. and 200 A.D. a Greek poet, Oppian, writing about the hunt, said:

"Tell then I pray....of those tribes of wild beasts which are of hybrid nature and mingled of two kinds, even the leopard of spotted back joined and united with the camel. Oh, Father Zeus, how many things has thou devised....even as thou has devised this varied form of the camel, clothing it with the hide of the shameless leopard, a race splendid and lovely and gentle to men. Long is its neck, its body spotted, the ears are small, the head is bare, the legs are long, the soles of the feet broad. From the middle of the head two horns rise straight up not horny but feeble projections on the head which alongside the ears rise up between the temples. The tender mouth is large, like that of a stag, and within are set on either side thin milk white teeth. A gleam lightens the eyes. The tail is short like that of the swift gazelles with dark hair at the end."

The best places in Africa to see giraffes today are in the northern province of Kenya, the great Serengeti plains of Tanzania, the Nairobi National Park (just five minutes out of the city of Nairobi) in Kenya, the Marsabit National Reserve in northern Kenya, Somalia, Tsavo National Park in southern Kenya, Amboseli National Reserve in southern Kenya and northern Tanzania. There are also fairly large herds in Kruger National Park in the Republic of South Africa.

It is not only conservationists in the African countries who are intent upon preserving the giraffe. Most of the African tribesmen are inclined to let it live out its life peacefully. There is some conflict for the land that has always been the native habitat of the giraffe and as the human population increases the great preserves are likely to shrink in size. Yet there is a good chance the giraffe will survive, if only because it does not need the valuable fertile lands but rather can find adequate food in the semiarid desert areas which are less useful to the expanding population.

The African people can look upon the giraffe not only as a distinctive animal but as a financial asset. For hundreds of giraffes are being shipped each year to the new kind of zoos that are developing in Europe and the Americas. These zoos, some commercial and others municipal, are similar to the animal reserves in Africa. Although seldom as extensive, the animals are not caged and move about the game preserves freely.

Of what use is a giraffe? It is an animal of great beauty and even of wonder—a triumph of nature. How large it is and yet how gentle! To see a giraffe in the cool highlands, with the purple-red African sun setting behind its tall, slim outline, is one of man's great visual experiences. Or to travel through the chill of an African dawn, and see the graceful outline of a herd of giraffes moving across the savanna, gives one a feeling of the world when it was new—when prehistoric beasts populated it.

Giraffes pay little attention to approaching vehicles. They are always curious but cautious.

GIRAFFES YESTERDAY TODAY AND TOMORROW

Like all mammals the giraffe's life consists of courtship, birth, maturity, old age and death. Because their life span is only 30 years, courtship begins when the animal is four years old.

During courtship male giraffes often touch the female. These are Reticulated giraffes in the Marsabit Reserve in Kenya's northern province.

In a gesture also used by the elephant when about to mate, a male giraffe lays his long

neck across the back of the female. Actual mating usually occurs in a secluded place.

△ *Ready to mate this handsome young Reticulated giraffe allows the male to lick her legs and her rump.*

◁ *A young male and female have moved into the privacy of the bush country to continue their courtship.*

Mostly plains animals, giraffes sometimes browse in forested areas. These are unusually dark in color. △
◁ *A young pregnant giraffe in Tanzania. It will take fifteen months from mating to calf's birth.*
Pregnant female giraffes are a common sight on the savannas of the Nairobi National Park in Kenya. ▽

◁ Giraffes and zebras are completely non-competitive. Zebras eat only grass, giraffes leaves and bark.

To reach a succulent herb this young giraffe must lean forward and spread his forelegs wide.

▽ Sharp thorns do not hurt the tough mouth of a giraffe. Its long muscular tongue quickly ejects them.

△ *Galloping giraffe raises front feet from the ground, then both back feet, in a rocking motion.*

◁ *By stretching its neck a full-grown giraffe can reach leaves twenty feet up in the treetops.*

Snow-capped Mount Kilimanjaro looms high above the heads of these two surprised Masai giraffes. ▷

THE ANATOMY
OF THE GIRAFFE

Almost every part of the giraffe has been designed by the evolutionary process for use and protection — the long neck, the strong legs, the hard head, the sinuous tongue. The two exceptions are his horns and tail. Neither of these appendages seem useful. The horns are left over from a previous ancestor, the prehistoric miniature deer known as *Cranioceras*. It, too, had a long graceful neck but its short horns were useful.

The giraffe's horns are not really horns at all. They have no relationship to the spreading antlers of the deer or the bone-like horns of cattle. No other animal has appendages quite like them. Both males and females have these short growths situated behind the eyes and rising from the top of the head. The giraffe is the only animal born with horns. At birth they are soft, covered with skin and long black hair, and are formed of cartilage, fiber and bone. By the time the male is two years old the horns have hardened and continue to grow and harden as the giraffe matures. The female's horns are lighter in weight and smaller in size. Older giraffes have hair growing in a circle around the horns.

Most giraffes have two of these appendages, but some of them have additional growths that form behind the ears and on the middle of the nose. The extra bump on the nose is particularly noticeable in the Reticulated giraffe. Early naturalists believed they were discovering a new species when they found giraffes with three, five and seven horns. Like the others, the additional "horns" are more like bumps that grow out from the skull. The five-horned giraffe, called the Baringo or Rothschild, has small bumps behind the ears, a horn like growth on the nose and the usual two horns.

Probably because the head of the giraffe gets knocked around considerably by hitting tree trunks accidentally and by hitting other giraffes on purpose, the skull continues to develop additional bone throughout most of its life. Between the time the giraffe is sexually mature at four years and the time it is 20 years old its skull may double in weight.

The tail of the giraffe is hardly long enough to brush away flies which, fortunately, do not seem to bother the giraffe as much as they do other animals. But, although the tail is not very useful, it has been responsible for the death of many giraffes. The tribesmen in a number of different countries of Africa have used its long black hairs as thread for stitching leather garments, have made fly whisks from it, as well as rings and amulets which are believed to bring good luck to the wearer. Before giraffes were as well protected as they are now, it was relatively common to find a dead giraffe with only its tail missing.

The neck of the giraffe, surprisingly enough, has the same number of vertebrae as the neck of a man or a horse, which is only seven. Its length is accounted for by the fact that each of these vertebrae is massive in size and they are hooked together by an intricate ball and socket skeletal structure. The front end of each bone is fitted into the concave end of the other, somewhat like the anatomy of a snake. But, unlike the snake, there are heavy ligaments and muscles between the vertebrae that hold the entire structure up. An elastic cartilage is present, not only in the neck of the giraffe but throughout its body, which lubricates and cushions the joints so well that it allows the large animal to move unusually smoothly. At times it seems to have springs in its joints.

The long neck of the giraffe is not always an asset. In some of the more developed areas of Africa giraffes have gotten into a good deal of trouble by walking into telephone, telegraph and electric wires strung on posts less than 18 feet high. It would be entirely possible for a giraffe to be electrocuted by the electric wire if it decided to chew on it.

The brain of the giraffe is relatively large. In his book *Animals as Social Beings*, Adolph Portmann claims that tests show the giraffe has the best organized brain information center of all of the cloven-hoofed animals. He rates its brain center (cerebrum) index as 29.5 compared to only 20 in wild cattle, such as the water buffalo, and twice as high as that of pigs, which he rates at only 14. But of course no one is really sure how clever giraffes are.

It was long thought the giraffe was mute, that they could not communicate with each other using sound, but recent research has proved this to be false. They can make a sound by pushing air through their long throat, which reminds one of the low mooing of a calf or the bleating of a sheep though not nearly as loud as either. The bull giraffe has been heard making a rasping noise something like a cough. Some observers think this could be a signal to the female. One other sound of the giraffe

has been recorded—that of a frightened young animal. It is similar to the bellow of the domestic calf often heard in the farmyard.

Only at mating time does the giraffe seem to use its sense of smell but it may be able to distinguish certain types of food by their odor.

The giraffe is truly a big-hearted animal for this organ is two feet long—approximately five times larger than the human heart. Its heart beats 150 times per minute, which is unusual, for generally the larger the heart the slower the beat. The lion has a heartbeat of 40, the elephant only 25, man between 70 and 80. But in all of these cases, elephant, man and lion, the heartbeat can and does increase with exercise and excitement. The giraffe seems geared for generally tranquil conditions for, even after running, its pulse does not go beyond 170, which is a very small increase.

Although there is only one genus of giraffe, there are many varieties, as there are different races of men. The races of giraffe are found in different parts of Africa and one scientist, Lydekker, has listed 10 subspecies. Most of them, however, are very much alike except for the Reticulated giraffe and what naturalists now call the Baringo or Rothschild. The most handsome of all is the Reticulated variety. This giraffe lives slightly north of the equator in East Africa in the northern province of Kenya. Beautiful examples of this type also occur in Somalia. The word reticulated refers to the markings which are like a network of white lines against a dark reddish-brown background. The distinctive pattern extends over its entire body.

The common giraffe, sometimes known as the Masai, is found mostly in mid-East Africa, although there are some in central, western and South Africa. The pattern of these giraffes is leaf-like, almost as though hundreds of small tree leaves were painted on their skin. The pattern is not as regular as that of the Reticulated. The common giraffe is known by many names in different parts of Africa. It is sometimes referred to as the Kilimanjaro, after the snow-capped mountain that rises 19,321 feet in northern

Rarest giraffe type is Rothschild. It has three to five distinct horny growths on its head.

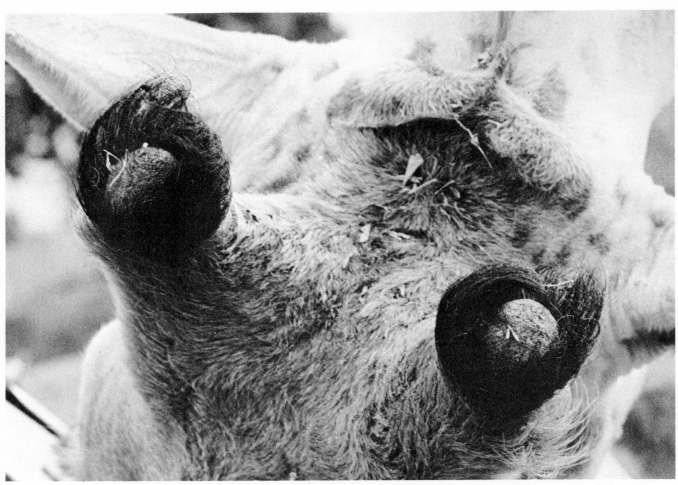

Unusual view shows giraffe head from above. Note hairs growing around the bony protuberances.
Hard hoof of the giraffe is well padded; its sharp bone-like structure can kill an adult lion.

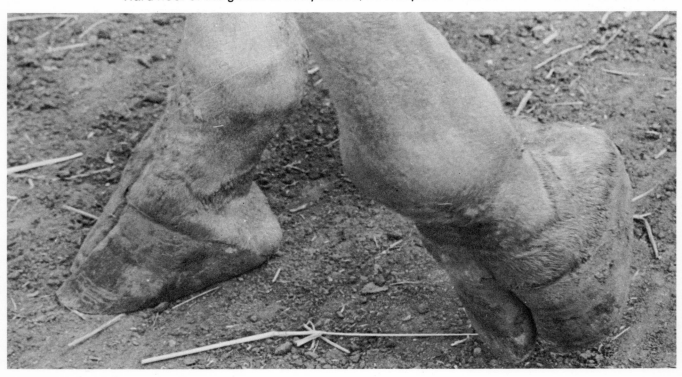

Tanzania. Giraffes are often seen in the foothills of this spectacular mountain where they climb to feed on the forested slopes.

The only relative of the giraffe is the okapi which we have mentioned before. While not as odd-looking as the giraffe, it too has some striking features. His coat is a reddish chestnut color which contrasts with his off-white face and throat. The rump and back legs are truly splendid for they are striped in alternating bands of black and white. The upper part of the front legs have stripes running completely around them. Each leg has a gray-white stocking with a black circle on the knee. You have to see it to believe it.

The okapi is much shorter than the giraffe, only about five and a half feet tall. The ears are very large, the neck medium long; and the only actual resemblance to the giraffe is in the length of its neck and the angle of its back. Unlike the giraffe, it lives in tropical forests. Most okapis are found in the upper Congo region of central Africa.

The okapi has even less family or herd spirit than the giraffe. It leads a lonely life singly, in pairs, or in very small groups. Fossil remains of the okapi show that it dates back in time as far, or farther, than the giraffe — at least 40,000 years. Today the okapi is rarer than the giraffe, even though it is seldom hunted except by the Pygmy people and professional animal trappers for the large zoos of the world.

It would be nice to say that a peaceful animal like the giraffe had no enemies but, unfortunately, this is not the case. Its five major enemies are the lion, the hyena, the leopard, man and a disease called rinderpest. Prides of lions prey only on old and feeble giraffes or attack very young ones that have strayed too far away from their mothers. Sometimes they stalk a cow when she is ready to give birth and are able to destroy both mother and off-spring. A few young giraffes may even be caught at water holes when they have spread their legs wide to get their muzzles into the water. But this hazard exists less for them than for other animals because the giraffe drinks less often. It gets most of its moisture from its food.

Hyenas operate in a different manner. They also work in packs but use speed and stamina to catch their prey rather than the stalking procedure used by the lions. If a young giraffe has strayed away, or an old bull or cow seems weak, the hyenas will run it down even if it takes hours. It is unlikely that hyenas do much damage to full-grown giraffes.

Leopards take the smallest group of young giraffes probably because there are not very many leopards left in Africa. They have been killed to produce leopard skin coats for so long that they are in danger of becoming extinct.

Man is considerably more dangerous to the giraffe than any of the above predators. Literally thousands of water buckets have been made from giraffe hide by African hunters. Giraffe sandals have been worn for generations. The meat of the giraffe, although not sought after as much as some of the smaller animals, is considered edible by many tribesmen. Before giraffes were well protected by law as they are now, many were hunted by farmers who objected to giraffes knocking down their fences and eating shrubs in their gardens.

But it is probable that a tiny, parasitic, disease-carrying organism called the rinderpest, or cattle plague, has killed more giraffes than all the other enemies combined. Yet this disease, which sometimes wipes out thousands of wildebeest and water buffalo, strikes the giraffe colonies more gently. The giraffes' system of living in small herds and keeping a healthy distance from one another may account for their survival from this disease. For the rinderpest is highly contagious. When it strikes a herd, it may kill half or more of its members.

How long do giraffes live? If the giraffe survives its enemies, and an increasing number of them do each year under the protection of the African governments, it will live to be between 20 and 35 years, about the lifetime of the average horse.

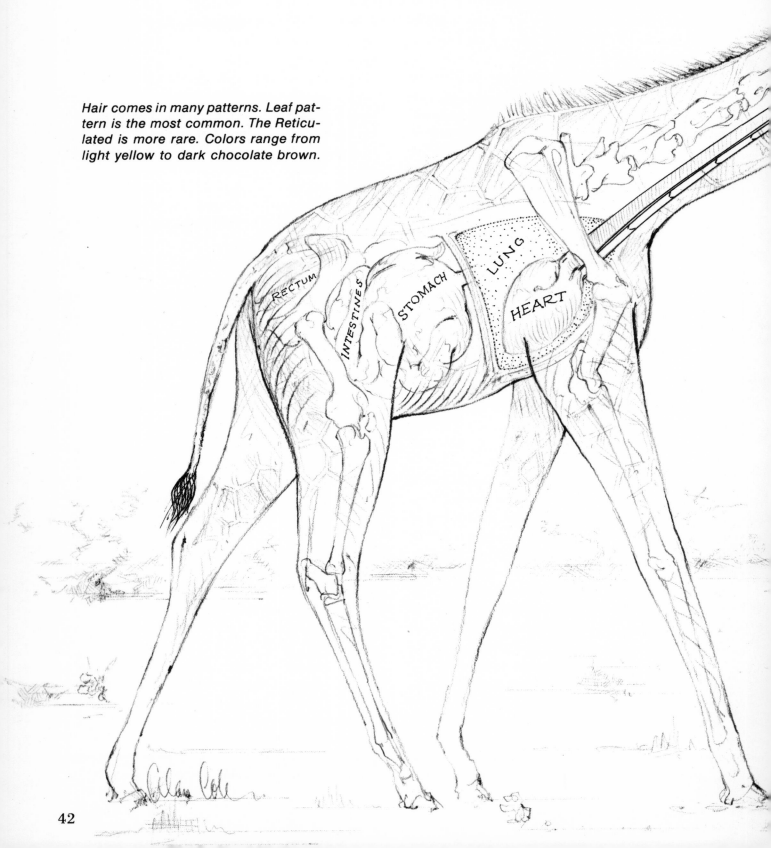

Skull is a unique cage-like bone structure. Brain is similar to that of horse or cow. It weighs 12 to 18 pounds and is well protected by the skull.

Hair comes in many patterns. Leaf pattern is the most common. The Reticulated is more rare. Colors range from light yellow to dark chocolate brown.

RECTUM

INTESTINES

STOMACH

LUNG

HEART

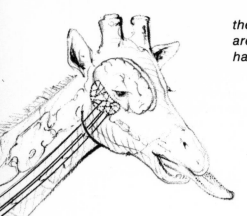

Horns are unique for giraffe is the only mammal born with them. They are a soft fibrous growth that becomes harder bone as the animal grows older.

Giraffe's eye has unusually large optic stalk that accounts for its extraordinary vision. It is known that giraffes have excellent color perception.

Tongue of giraffe is long (up to 18 inches) and muscular. It is flexible enough at the tip to grasp twigs and branches and expel inedible objects.

Neck has only seven vertebrae, the same as man. Its short backbone, combined with its long legs, makes the neck appear much longer than it is.

INSIDE THE GIRAFFE

20 QUESTIONS AND ANSWERS

1. *What is the giraffe's scientific name, order, suborder and family?*

The *Giraffa camelopardalis Brisson* belongs to the *Artiodactyla* order, the *Ruminantia* suborder and is a member of the *Giraffidae* family. Man belongs to the *Primate* order, *Anthropoidea* suborder and the *Hominidae* family.

2. *How far back in time have we found evidence of the giraffe's existence?*

For at least twenty-five million years, although we are constantly finding new evidence which changes our dating. Man has existed for approximately twenty million years, give or take a few million either way.

3. *Does the giraffe have any relatives?*

Yes, the okapi. Its fossil remains date back at least as far as, or perhaps further than, the giraffe. But it is now much rarer than the giraffe in Africa.

4. *What is the favorite food of the giraffe?*

It prefers the high growing leaves of the mimosa and acacia trees. When necessary, by spreading its front legs, it can get its neck down and reach plants near or on the ground.

5. *Why has the giraffe not been domesticated?*

What for? The milk cannot be drunk, it cannot be easily led, and riding its sloping back would be impossible.

6. *Do giraffes drink much water?*

No, in its hot, dry home in Africa a giraffe may go weeks when it is necessary without drinking water. It obtains all the moisture it needs from the leaves it eats. In a zoo it drinks about two gallons a week.

7. *Is the giraffe the world's tallest animal?*

Yes, it may grow as tall as 18-1/2 feet but 16 feet is the average height for an adult.

8. *How fast can a giraffe run?*

It can run up to 32 miles an hour, outrunning a horse for short distances.

9. *How soon after birth is the giraffe able to walk or run?*

A giraffe can keep up with the herd at any speed, even running, a few hours after birth.

10. *How large is a giraffe's heart?*

About two feet long, which is longer than the average human baby at birth.

11. *Would it be fair to describe the giraffe as boneheaded?*

Yes, its head develops additional bone throughout most of its life. Between the ages of four and 20 years its skull doubles in weight.

12. *How many vertebrae are there in a giraffe's neck?*

Seven, the same number all mammals have, but the giraffe's bones are larger.

13. *Do giraffes ever sleep lying down?*

Yes, with its neck either held straight out or bent back enabling the head to rest on the body. These creatures never sleep for more than a few minutes at a time.

14. *At what times are giraffes in most danger?*

When they are sleeping and when the female is having her calf.

15. *Do giraffes fight among themselves?*

Fighting and sparring is common between male giraffes but the blows are seldom heavy and the combatants often rub necks between bouts. Serious fights are less common.

16. *Do giraffes use their hoofs for defense?*

Yes, they use their powerful hoofs to defend themselves and their young and even the most dangerous beast of prey can be injured by one single blow.

17. *To what practical use has man put the giraffe?*

The live animal has been of no use to man except for its beauty. But his hide, tail and flesh have proved valuable for making water buckets, sandals, whips and for food.

18. *Is the giraffe's future in danger because of civilization approaching its natural habitats?*

Not as much as most animals. Although the land available to giraffes has been reduced, they do not require potentially fertile farm areas for finding their food. Native crops are not threatened by giraffes as they are by grass-eating animals.

19. *Are giraffes happy in zoos?*

Nobody knows, but giraffes mate, breed and raise their young in zoos everywhere.

20. *Do most giraffes look alike?*

No, there are at least 10 different color varieties and every individual giraffe has a slightly different skin pattern.

ACKNOWLEDGEMENTS

This is my sketchbook of observations in Africa and research work in England and the United States devoted to the giraffe. It would take many volumes and thousands of photographs to completely contain the evolution, history, anatomy, herd life and ecology of this fascinating animal. These pages, then, are an introduction to the tallest of the land mammals.

Most of the work on the book was done in the East African countries of Kenya, Tanzania and Uganda. In each I received advice and help and I wish now to offer my thanks to the following people and institutions. In Kenya I am indebted to Mr. and Mrs. Jack Block who made my stay at their New Stanley Hotel a very pleasant one. I shall never forget the Thorne Tree Terrace of the New Stanley which is the African crossroads meeting place where old and new Africa hands exchange stories and information. It was here that I met Mr. and Mrs. Monty Ruben (he is the co-producer of the important film "The African Elephant") and Simon Trevor, the talented motion picture cameraman who photographed it.

I was welcomed at all of the national parks and game reserves. My thanks to the efficient wardens and gamekeepers of Samburu Game Reserve, Kilimanjaro Game Reserve, Mount Kenya National Park, Nairobi National Park, Serengeti National Park, Tsavo National Park, Masai-Amboseli Game Reserve, Lake Manyara National Park, Ngorongoro Crater National Park. I am especially grateful to Mr. H. G. T-Russell, Director of Tanzania National Parks, and Mr. P. M. Olindo, Director of the Kenya National Parks. In Uganda I traveled from Entebbe to Kasese and Mweya where I photographed the hippopotamus in the Kazinga Channel which joins Lakes George and Edward. More hippos were observed and photographed in Murchison Falls National Park where the Nile River acts as host to hippos, crocodiles, elephants, kob and buffalo. My thanks also to Barbara and Gordon Evans who drove me back from Murchison Falls to Kampala when air reservations became unprocurable.

In England the library of the British Museum proved helpful and in the United States I had the pleasure of consulting with Mr. Norman Myers (who lives in Nairobi and is a photographer-writer on Africa). Also in the United States I received the cooperation of Mr. Frederick Childress, Director of Information and Education, and other members of the staff of the San Diego Zoo. Before I left for Africa, my friend Jim Moran had thoughtfully provided me with introductions to the Blocks and Rubens of Nairobi. The executives of Lion Country Safari in Laguna Hills, California, have always been helpful. Finally, I want to express my thanks to my colleague Jerry Cooke who accompanied me on this African safari.

Bradley Smith
La Jolla, California

BIBLIOGRAPHY

Aristotle, *History of Animals*, Transl. by R. Creswell. London: George Bell and Sons, 1907.

Breasted, J. A., *A History of Egypt*. London: Hodder and Stoughton, 1906.

Bridges, William and Mary Baker, *Wild Animals of the World*. New York: Garden City Books, 1948.

Brown, Leslie, *Africa: A Natural History*. New York: Random House, 1965.

Cloudsley-Thompson, J. L., *Animal Behavior*. New York: The Macmillan Company, 1961.

Cloudsley-Thompson, J. L., *Animal Conflict and Adaptation*. London: G. T. Foulis & Co., Ltd., 1965.

Dagg, A. I., *Giraffe Movement and the Neck*, National History Magazine, Vol. 71, New York, 1962.

Engel, Fritz-Martin, *Life Around Us*. New York: Thomas Y. Crowell Co., 1965.

Foster, J. B., *The Giraffe of Nairobi National Park: Home Range, Sex Ratios, the Herd, and Food*, East African Wildlife Journal, Vol. 4, Nairobi, 1966.

Goodall, E., et al., *Prehistoric Rock Art of Rhodesia and Nyasaland*, Salisbury: National Publications Trust, 1959.

Herodotus, *Histories*. Transl. by H. Carter. London: Oxford University Press, 1962.

Jennison, G., *Animals for Show and Pleasure in Ancient Rome*. Manchester: Manchester University Press, 1937.

Laufer, B., *The Giraffe in History and Art*. Chicago: Field Museum of Natural History, 1928.

Lawrence, W. E., and R. E. Rewell, *The Cerebral Blood Supply in the Giraffidae*. Proceedings of the Zoological Society #118, London, 1948.

Life Editors and Barnett, Lincoln, *The World We Live In*. New York: Time Inc., 1955.

Michelmore, Susan, *Sexual Reproduction*. New York: The Natural History Press, 1965.

Morris, Desmond, *The Mammals*. New York: Harper & Row, 1965.

Myers, Norman, *The Long African Day*. Ms. notes.

Park, Mungo, *The Travels*. London: J. M. Dent, 1960.

Parrinder, Geoffrey, *African Mythology*. London: Paul Hamlyn, 1967.

Pliny, *Natural History*. Transl. by H. Rackham. London: William Heinemann, 1952.

Sidney, J., *Distribution of African Ungulates*. London Zoological Society. Transactions, Vol. 30, 1965.

Spinage, C. A., *The Book of the Giraffe*. London: Collins, 1968.

White, T. H., *The Book of Beasts*. London: Jonathan Cape, 1954.

Zeuner, F. E., *A History of Domesticated Animals*. New York: Harper & Row, 1963.

INDEX

A

Abyssinian, 13
Acacia, 16
Africa, 37-38, 41, 43
   East Africa, 38
   North Africa, 42
   South Africa, 38, 43
Amboseli National Reserve, 12, 43
America, 43
Animals as Social Beings, 38
Antelope, 21
Anthropoidea, 44
Arabia, 20
Arabs, 13
Artiodactyla, 13, 44
Asia, 42-43

B

Brisson, Mathurin Jacques, 13

C

Caesar, Julius, 42
California, 24
Camel, 13, 16
Camelopardalis, 13
Carnivore, 16, 18
Cervus camelopardalis, 13
Cheetah, 20
China, 42-43
Congo, 41
Cow, 17
Cranioceras, 37

D

Deer, 14, 37, 42
Dog, 17

E

Egyptians, 42
Elephant, 13, 16, 19, 21, 38, 42
Ethiopian, 13
Europe, 42-43

F

France, 43
Frederick II, Emperor, 42

G

Gazelle, 21, 42
Giraffa camelopardalis Brisson, 13, 44

Giraffe
   ancestors, 37
   Baringo, 37
   birth, 17, 41, 44
   brain, 38
   bull, 16-17, 19-21, 37-38
   calf, 5, 8-11, 13, 16-19, 37
   classification, 13
   communication, 38
   courtship, 17, 26-29
   cow, 17-20, 30-31, 37
   defense, 18, 20, 42, 44
   description, 13
   digestion, 14
   drinking, 16, 41, 44
   ears, 14
   ecology, 43, 45
   enemies, 16-17, 41
   evolution, 14, 18, 37, 42, 44
   eyes, 13-15
   eyesight, 16-17
   feeding, 14, 16, 20, 33-35, 44
   fighting, 19-20, 44
   food, 14, 16
   gait, 17, 20, 34, 44
   gestation, 17
   hair, 37, 40
   head, 16, 20, 37, 44
   heart, 38, 44
   height, 13, 17-18, 44
   herd, 19
   history, 42-43
   hoofs, 40, 44
   horns, 37, 39-40
   hunting, 37, 41-42
   intelligence, 19
   legend, 42
   legs, 20, 37
   life span, 41
   lips, 14, 16
   Masai, 35, 38
   milk, 17, 42, 44
   neck, 13, 16-17, 20-21, 37-38
   nose, 14, 17
   nursing, 5, 17-18
   olfactory, 38
   pattern, 21, 38

pulse, 38
Reticulated, 25, 37-38
Rothschild, 37, 39
saliva, 16
sexual behavior, 17-18, 28-29, 38
skin, 13, 16, 42
sleeping, 20, 44
sounds, 38
stomach, 13-14
tail, 37
teats, 17
teeth, 14
territory, 20
tongue, 14, 16, 37
vertebrae, 38, 44
weight, 17-18
Giraffid, 42
Giraffidae, 13, 44
Greece, 13
Greek, 13, 43

H

Herbivore, 16
Hominidae, 44
Horse, 17, 19-20, 38, 41-42
Hyena, 13, 17, 41

I

Impala, 21
India, 42
Italy, 43

J

Johnson, Dr. Samuel, 13

K

Kenya, 12, 16, 21, 25, 38, 43
Kilimanjaro, 35, 38
Kruger National Park, 43

L

Legend, 20
Leopard, 13, 17, 41
Linnaeus, Carolus, 13
Lion, 13-14, 16-17, 21, 38, 41
Lion Country Safari, 21
Lydekker, R., 38

M

Madagascar, 43
Marco Polo, 43
Marsabit National Reserve, 25, 43
Medici, Lorenzo de, 43
Mediterranean, 42

Michelangelo, 43
Mongolia, 42
Myers, Norman, 19

N

Nairobi National Park, 21, 31, 43
Nairobi University College, 21

O

Okapi, 13
   description, 41
   fossils, 41, 44
   habitat, 41
   habits, 41
Oppian, 43

P

Persia, 42
Pig, 13, 38
Portmann, Adolph, 38
Primate, 44
Pygmy people, 41

R

Rinderpest, 41
Rome, 42
Ruminant, 13-14
Ruminantia, 13, 44

S

Sahara Desert, 42
Serengeti Plains National Park, 43
Sheep, 38
Snake, 38
Somalia, 38, 43
Sultan of Egypt, 43

T

Tanzania, 41, 43
Thorn tree, 14, 16
Tsavo National Park, 43

U

Ungulate, 13, 42
University College, 21

W

Water buffalo, 38, 41
Wildebeest, 21, 41

Z

Zarafah, 13
Zarat, 13
Zebra, 21, 33
Zoological Society of London, 43